BUGS & BEETLES

BEETLES

By William Anthony

BookLife
PUBLISHING

©2019
BookLife Publishing Ltd.
King's Lynn
Norfolk, PE30 4LS

ISBN: 978-1-78637-724-1

Written by:
William Anthony

Edited by:
John Wood

Designed by:
Amy Li

QR by:
Kelby Twyman

A catalogue record for this book is available from the British Library.

All facts, statistics, web addresses and URLs in this book were verified as valid and accurate at time of writing. No responsibility for any changes to external websites or references can be accepted by either the author or publisher.

All rights reserved. Printed in Malaysia.

To use the QR codes in this book, make sure you set one of these apps as your default browser. If you don't know how to do this, ask an adult to help you!

- Chrome
- Safari
- Firefox
- Ecosia

Your QR app might open the links in this book straight away, but if it doesn't, always click on the button that says something like 'open', 'continue', 'browse' or something similar.

PHOTO CREDITS – Images/videos are courtesy of Shutterstock.com. With thanks to Getty Images, Thinkstock Photo and iStockphoto.

Cover – Nik Merkulov, Karramba Production, Ermak Oksana, ten43, azure1, aodaodaodaod, Aggie 11, hardik s panchal, Imageman, irin-k, Michael Potter11, Protasov AN, Tiplyashina Eveniya. Recurring Images – ten43, THPStock (paper), aodaodaodaod (header texture), Simon Bratt (main background), Robert Biedermann (vector beetles in header), Karramba Productions (parchment), Andrey Eremin, Steve Paint (labels), azure1 (magnifying glass), Dacian G (vector phone), Ortis, Nella, Imageman, Aggie 11 (page decoration), Ermak Oksana (doodles). P1 – Nik Merkulov, p2-3 – Sergio MF, p4-5 – szefei, Dmitry Naumov, Martin Grossman (web), p6-7 – Marek Rybar, Stefan Rotter, p8-9 – Mark Brandon, Czesnak Zsolt, Diedov Denys (video), p10-11 – vblinov, JUN3, p12-13 – Diyana Dimitrova, Igor Chus, Pronghorn Productions (video), p14-15 – MIkhail Gnatovskiy, Michael Potter11, naturewatch (video), p16-17 – Rudmer Zwerver, Jan Mastnik, p18-19 – Stuart G Porter, pusit_panya, p20-21 – Petr Simon, Eric Isslee, Smile Studio, p22-23 – Hatchapong Palurtchaivong, StockSmartStart, Mike McDonald, p24 – Nik Merkulov

CONTENTS

Words that look like **THIS** can be found in the glossary on page 24.

EXPLORER TRAINING

Hey, over here! We need your help. Our team of explorers really needs a new member. Do you think you could do the job? First, we'll need to train you up.

This book uses videos to teach you all about beetles. Just use your phone or tablet to scan the QR codes that you see throughout this book.

Try scanning this code to test if your explorer equipment is working. Can you see the photo on your device?

If you don't have one already, ask an adult to download a free QR code scanner from wherever you usually get your apps!

WHAT IS A BEETLE?

First up, we need to know about each part of a beetle. Beetles are a type of insect. Insects have no backbones and have six legs attached to their bodies.

The three main parts of an insect's body are the head, the thorax and the abdomen.

Head

Thorax

Abdomen

Antennae

Longhorn beetle

Beetles have two antennae attached to their heads. These can be very short or very long. Sometimes they are called feelers because they help the beetle to **SENSE** what is around them.

ADAPTATIONS

Rhinoceros beetle

Like other bugs, beetles have **ADAPTED** in lots of ways. Many beetles have two sets of wings. Their front wings are hardened cases that protect their soft back wings, which are used for flying.

They lift up their hard front wings before stretching out their soft back wings and flying away. Beetles that can't fly have two sets of hard wings, which make it too difficult to fly.

Quick! Scan the QR code before the beetle flies away...

HOME LIFE

Beetles can be found on every **CONTINENT** on the planet, except Antarctica. Beetles have adapted to live in many different **HABITATS**. Different beetles can live in places that are hot, cold, wet or dry.

Darkling beetles can be found in hot, dry deserts such as the Namib desert in Africa.

Stag beetles live underground while they are still **LARVAE**.

Beetles across the world have many different types of homes. Some beetles burrow themselves deep underground, while others live in trees. A beetle's home depends on the type of habitat they live in.

FINDING A FEAST

Colorado potato beetles get their name from their favourite food – potato plants!

Most beetles are herbivores. This means they eat plant parts, such as the stem or the fruit. Some beetles are omnivores. This means they eat both plants and other animals, such as maggots or earthworms.

Beetles have several mouthparts. Most have two jaws that work like scissors to chop up plants. They also have small palps, which are like small antennae that act as fingers to help the beetles hold their food.

Jaws

Palps

Look — another QR code! Scan it to get up close to a beetle eating.

DUNG BEETLES

There is one type of beetle that prefers a different **DIET** – the dung beetle. Dung beetles eat poo! First, they collect and move other animals' poo by making it into a ball and rolling it.

The Egyptian **SACRED** scarab is a type of dung beetle.

Dung beetles roll the poo by standing behind the ball on their front legs and pushing it with their back legs.

There's another QR code! Scan it to watch the dung beetle pushing its poo ball.

TEAMWORK

Dung beetles are also good at working as a team. Male and female dung beetles work in pairs to collect as many poo (dung) balls as they can. They will even fight off other dung beetles for the poo.

Male and female beetles work as a pair to roll dung balls to a safe place.

This dung beetle larva has eaten its way through the dung ball.

When the pair are safe from other animals, the female lays a single egg in the dung ball. This gives the young larva enough food to survive when it hatches, helping it grow into an adult.

STAYING SAFE

Beetles can be **PREY** for many other larger animals. Some animals that eat beetles are birds, bats, frogs and even other insects. However, some beetles know how to fight back.

Bombardier
beetle

Bombardier beetles have a secret weapon in their abdomen. They can spray a boiling, painful **LIQUID** at attackers to stop them trying to eat them.

BONKERS BEETLES

Male stag beetles have two long jaws that they wrestle each other with. They might fight over females or food.

Quick! Scan the QR code to see some beetles having a wrestling match.

Some beetles can grow to huge sizes. The Hercules beetle can grow to a size of up to 18 centimetres long.

Actual size!

TIME TO EXPLORE

Well, that's the end of your training. Good news – you've passed! You are now ready to go out and explore the wilderness, armed with your new knowledge. But there's one more thing you'll need before you go...

...your well-earned explorer's badge! Scan the final QR code below to download your very own Beetle Expert Badge. Print it off, cut it out and wear it with pride. Congratulations, explorer!

GLOSSARY

adapted	changed over time to fit with the environment
continent	a very large area of land, such as Africa or Europe, that is made up of many countries
diet	the kinds of food that an animal usually eats
habitats	the natural homes in which animals or plants live
larvae	young insects that must grow and change before they reach their adult form
liquid	a material that flows, such as water
prey	animals that are hunted by other animals for food
sacred	to do with religion and worship
sense	to feel or be aware of

INDEX